On the Raft with Fr. Roseliep

James Liddy

On the Raft with Fr. Roseliep

ARLEN
HOUSE

First published in April 2006 by Arlen House

PO Box 222
Galway
Ireland
Phone/fax: 353 86 8207617
Email: arlenhouse@gmail.com

ISBN 1–903631–83–1, *paperback*

Printed by ColourBooks, Dublin
Typesetting by Arlen House

CONTENTS

ACKNOWLEDGEMENTS

Some of these poems first appeared in: *The Black Mountain Review, Donkey Jaw, The Dodo Bird, The Irish Times, Triquarterly, Woodland Pattern Poetry Anthology No. 11, The Recorder, Eddie's Own Aquarius, An Sionnach.*

for Jeff and Scott

'This album is dedicated to, and is for and about the death of the sweetheart. In a social plane, impossible to exist, and in memories, past defeating present. We mourn the sweetheart's loss ...'

– Jack White

LET'S INVADE OURSELVES NOT IRAQ

Professor, are you thinking of retirement?
I haven't fully explored the drinking age yet.

I have a crusade inside me against killing in war
astonishing for a drinking man;
Sweetheart, I have a crusade in me that steams like a
    decaying liver
towards you.
I refill an observation:
writing & university currently sobered up with
    schoolmarms
going by the book. Invade bottled water.

Autobiography whispers in Cleopatra's ear noble
    unencumbered woman
what would happen if we weren't failures?
Should victory stay in the closet?
A roll in my pub and sullen art,
barman in Davy Byrne's door says, 'Good morning, Sir?'
I lay agenbite of inwit beside the glass.
Mars, have mercy, direct wars within.

Enrafted In Wexford

I made it up to Spawell Road
to the reconstructing Memorial Park
to pray to the whereabouts of Willie Redmond
the rumpled humble loser
drinker with priests long ago in Co. Clare –

a Park Place butterfly
soprano in neck shakes:
in the sun before I got on the plane
I knew she was welcoming; Clare,
waltz pleasure.

I wander from Nora's house
to where I can see trees St. Peter's:
a snatch of a reading
a hundred sweet boiling young men
heads over soutanes alerted to imagery,
too earthly an image of Paradise?

Long hand-shaking, going on the town 'like girls.'
Orpheus noted them
and they danced:
rocks, stones, branches,
choristers in the street,
carol singers on walls and hills
priests on bad dream nights:
Jeff, Scott.

There ought to be more Masses
said by lay people for the dead,
we would sing in choir
they would come into the choir.

You must go on this raft
the way down the river
your mother and priests
drinking and talking on it,
changing their clothes
like you will from good to
bad, the river decides.

ON THE RAFT WITH FR. RAYMOND ROSELIEP

I've been to St. Louis many times
Prufrock's breath
drained in the Welsh bar

The brown river god thinks
as I do
on all the separation

water-run trunks
of boys and men
dry in their catechisms

landings in clouds
want to turn cash in July

no love boats from Russia
only a cargo of apples

teach teachers how
to drink cider in public

those who put
arms around me or almost hug
I never put my arms round them

William sweet William
let me choose in the dust
miracle of the water rat

Father I'm not afraid of Virginia
I'm afraid of Leonard
who could swim by that man

I stretch my legs
sun on your belly
sun on my belly

I carve out of the river a little
America that tells it's a loan

Fr. Roseliep throws haikus off the raft
in the long bends
a Fire Island is waiting

O little Rome of the muse
I am a fondling dogma
drifting down river.

NIEDECKER'S MUSEUM, MILWAUKEE

I

You got a raw deal
you said to yourself
Muse/Museum says
no deal is better son

II

Dreamt on these walls
future's furniture
nip it into you

III

From Morris Graves's
oiseau to another
without sleeplessness

IV

Baseball caps
underneath Mozart-randy
Bukowski in their pockets

V

Opposite of a soccer field
but plenty of moms
plus solitude's androgeny

VI

Le coq de la Liberation 1944
cet
no nebulae

VII

Everyone is half cute
in an art museum

VIII

Hold your heart
Rothko's shell or house
of windows

IX

Starved for typewriters
they played marbles
on rivers' doors

X

Step on Avery's river boat
Darwin Morris Yeats on board
like a supper club

XI

From pillar to post
in a glass menagerie
of grasshoppers (drinks)

XII

Should be drunk as a pet shop boy
LN on wild green arts and letters
parsing them
and molest the cocktail shaker

XIII

Gail Roub should we be sure
America moves
a 'golden futurite vessel'

XIV

On this coast and crossroads
the god Hermes holds
his workshop
two A's in the class
Watt and Niedecker

BLACK HAWK ISLAND
9/17/05 to Jonathan Williams

She liked the Enlightenment
she liked cabbage.

What America needs
is not more cars in
church parking lots
but in a rural setting
a non-Christian poet.

(Lorine's bio)
no kiss from Louis
careerless.

I was officially loved
by some in the world
thus not without merit
but disdain for others
was tornado-dark.

The waltz was lovely
not slow, danceable and
sprayable on water.

Migration to Club 26
supper club of pirates

bathtub gin makers
toy boys free rounds!

WHO KILLED PATRICK KAVANAGH?
Milwaukee Service, October 2004

Who killed Patrick Kavanagh?
I said the Ombudsman with my bow and paper.

Brought up under daily cafe shadow, my ghost.

Voice of Cantor, *Tea and biscuit poet, scotch and scotch poet.*

Ignorance liberated is poetry.

Voice of Cantor, *If he is 'Wanton.'*

He post-Renaissance copy book image. June to September
   Professors
came from the airport, swallows in summer heat to
   libraries Mrs.
Yeats Liam Miller, briefly and doubtfully surveyed his
   haunts.

Voice of Cantor, *Cold swallows in summer heat.*

Who killed James Joyce who killed Patrick Kavanagh the
   latter an
inside job.

Voice of Cantor, *Do ye want to be orphans, first duty of any
   kid
is fuck the English teacher.*

21

We all arrive at the gate the bar dates, which hot
    gospeller
hidden in the flaming abergut?

Voice of Cantor, *Dedalus was straight kid Rimbaud queer kid,
    who
rocked the boats on the river higher?*

Do you hear the ghosts scream along the Seine, 'Nous
accusons.'

Voice of Cantor, *Peace & romance.*

Pray for us now and at the hour of our publication.

CLOCHARDS DANCE

An Irish boy on the road looking for dances, or dancers.

He finds his church hunched in madness – continuing,
    growing – at
Mass Rock up the road, shadow has no end.

The Rock rebirth – slow word mince won't do, first step
    wild in the ditch with
broken melodeon. You have time to pour yourself in
    stone choreography.

Hunted Latin words ... the priests were not instructors in
    stone, they were agents.

People dance, people dance on the mad road ... in my
    arms pulsate with my struggle,
pastel hues, twig and fug in costume. Rebirth partner, let
    limbs be sorted out
on the Mass Rock love site if you keep time. Sweet
    ribcage, this beauty lying in the dirt.
What if he is a character in a Rock Opera?

Have we mastered the paperback dance, the Purgatory
road, after we've been introduced to the disease of
gender? We jog on the road, we read stars and maps, it's
a question of what restaurants to inhabit. Music traded

for menu, kids entwine with saints: what is your film the
interviewer asks and the dancers mime, 'An expression of
our profound, intimate, Catholicism.'

The scene or scent of boys keeping to electric rock, that
belongs to the ancient world,
birth going round and round in restaurant mirrors.
Nimbus a-shaking ...
you dance a lot you don't cool off. A hit. Song of yourself.

Ar Chreag i Lár na Farraige

In the middle of the Ocean

Fishing in the summer, painting in the autumn, fucking
winters, gorgeous island.

Their hearts were fine in the wild winds, not writers,
    painters.

They would go into the waves, kick the fish to the pier or
    rocks.

If you went too far and started drowning they wouldn't
    help, the sea
was taking you back.

They knew Derek Hill's cottage on the hill was stacked
    with liquor,
their spoils as liberators.

Toasts to the King of the island.

Women, what women, they were like men.

When islanders married they stayed with father mother
    brother and sister,
they weren't like Christian people, the Parish Priest got
    cross said no
to the keys to the school for a social, there was no hall.

The girls walked from one end of the place to the other
      remembering songs,
wanting attention.

The boys walked from one end of the place to the other
      remembering songs,
wanting attention.

Shaky sweet voices on the outskirts of revelation.

Tory, in one way or another, knelt a high priest.

VICTOR WADDINGTON'S

Fergus my friend outside the Physics Theatre,
we wander to the galleries, I tell the story
of Black Pat Bolger from Camolin:
had to wait an hour for the dentist
went in and bought a Yeats painting.

We are outside Victor Waddington's

violent violet blues and greens
cloth of wash figures shine, suit of late
evening and lake light, the wild horse
of the night in last daylight,
living daylight blown into everything
coming highlight in cloudy sherry carousal,
rainbow in low praising fields unseen
outside the studio, stained glass
in provenance sudden silhouette
single blaze. Spirits such as they are
sun-hopping under the cloud barges
pour insides out on tempest
winds struck in the grass,
saint's matchstick limb haloed
by the bell knocking the hill,
the glory horses have started ...

is within swimming distance
green blue distance a suit of light again,

we have to bow to the manure
of shade and shadow
night or day or no night and no day.

The understated bullfight in Ulster
taurine landscape dissolving to us

we enter a Celtic twilight for the first time
that is not on the page I say to Fergus –

Fergus the student of classics replies,
I prefer the prayer of Odysseus.

THE TREE OF WHICH

Ten miles from the village
by the Slate Quarry road
The Meeting of the Waters.
That is our reward.
Isn't that enough? The Avonbeg
the Avonmore and Avoca.
I saw the river at
Arklow abandoned schooners.

I saw how Wicklow worked
its ships its fisheries its shawls
and for my ancestors of
distant Clare and Limerick
I include references to O Brudair
in poems about Moore
but hey we lay under the tree
free thinking in our own way.

O Brudair the 17th century poet
who is translated by Michael Hartnett
who just got off the Transatlantic phone.
That's alright but let me lie under
the tree and savor what Moore wrought:
the English language part of Irish freedom.
Isn't it enough, that sweeping sweetness?

AISLINGI

Kay Boyle/Frank O' Connor's daughter
hitchhiking among lorries, 'Is there a phone near here
we need to ring Co. Wexford.'

NOBEL GOLD

Into the valley of James Joyce rode the 600 metaphors
that should have been dervishes.

Sweet rain water in Northern Ireland
so the horses offered to drink it when they came
to the stream of the island inside the island.

Harvard never existed only horses do.
The clouds came to Boston and begged to flower,
damp heaving on asteroid hooves.

Honey mixed with water so landscape became as luscious
as a tinted photograph.
Stoned horses levitation mellifluence water.

They store our gold in Scandinavia and pay interest
but we are on a different plateau: Yeats's platonic
dolls Joyce's horny toy fair, fun beauty.

Stolen goods, collars of gold and
libations? Libation of dervishes, hold out your glass.

Ambulance,
nursing home and funeral parlor in one –
'linkboys' my escorts with candles,
'moon-men' ahead of my carriage
support your poles topped by lanterns.

Opaque?

Can love
the giant question

It is a conspiracy of giants
serial

We do not imitate think again

work with what
happens to you there is no other happiness

I'm tired of world music I want to travel
to the city of destruction
so we can confront it

sing in my chains like you sing in your chains

that you are a beautiful man and all that
fingers playful as rabbits touched with sorrow (rabbit
     once in
this writing)
orderly infection

I dream back to kindergarten
(invented in Wisconsin)
hand in hand up the first path to the door
to the first door escape from mother

finger in finger
car float

Not living anymore than we did but deep things keep
    audible

I stumble in and out of sleep
type up queries

I have just eaten Serbian sweetbreads with you
and read Robert Duncan what book do your hands hold
what are you doing this week
(all love is two questions)

GERMAN-AMERICAN DRIVING

A lovely white car
drivers in colours
you have a black shirt over your chest

let us drape our shirts on the wheel as we set off

Chest and shoulders in a soldier's shirt
styles are a storm of blood
passing the speed limit is victory
there are dust and potholes

and there is the music 'Speeding for love'
on the sudden car radio

Lost St. Christopher medals everywhere

St. Christopher the designated driver
no other saint hangs late in the town
whistle 'free zone'

We rented cars and roared

you a Hot Holy Hill rod
white soul in a white body
behind a white car's wheel

I was a highway I bowed
I was a four lane general I raised my hand

I hear archaic echoes of
'I love trains I hate Henry Ford'

time a white horse zone memory
Keith in black shirt bellhops the wheel

Tracks
in Wagner Town
fast thick and known
first autobahn is last autobahn

ON A MODEL
(JOSE DE CIRIA Y ESCALANTE)

Who saw you, what time did I?
Twilight is a strange pudding.
Noises – the alarm clock
wind-shadow. First sun
in the window ignores you.

Too much butter-like incensed
water invests your head:
Male form! Crush! Wakelight!
Manhood on the moon as
everything is made from nothing.

Beautiful lunar plant, slip into
my controversy of pain,
I pull a silver apple out of a poem
and slide it in the jet steam
of reddened fishermen-tourists.

O you up there on a green
peopleless oasis, don't bother
about weeping if you are able,
not over this vast fucked-up place,
lowkey thrilling Giocondo, my sweet.

– from Lorca

PROCEDURES FOR BOB WATT'S 80TH

I

An owl sat on the Schlitz sign
remember hooting?

Sex is the sole Utopia
no brains are used.

Must not stop typing
poem museshining women

to have a soul as shiny
as a piece of Sendiks fruit.

Warm night students hooting
2 a.m. Oakland to North.

Moon half
Landmark Lanes full –

II

Say real laws
the kind that Plato
taught should be footnotes
but the wind touched them
outside the cave and made them punk,
nubile laws like nights
out in the red or pink light district
(My hearties sex is a field joke.)

Everyone wants to be Baudelaire
once they've read his journal
he was a bitch on golden wheels
an idol scrambled by history's lava,
Bob Watt drives around in a car
designed by Matisse from the grave
that working people admire
the flowers on the roof
are wilted they began on the Left Bank.
Humming as if he is near the Seine
in the Irish Quarter not the Irish College
Watt is Parisian.
His ancestor lies in Kilrush
mine up in Killydysert,
we were priests a reincarnation ago
we hid in the bog with that bit of God
that makes plans now.
We stroll motley troubadours
at the corner of Oakland and Locust
who dwelt in the sports
of the god of love when we were young
and it was fashionable. Cabaret. Get to it.

III

My birthday speech
mon saboteur

Pain in a sailor's veil
uneconomic butterfly

such stuff
our dreams are bent with

Not of legal age
I'll go out buy anything

flirt
spend bucks

Sandwich heart
reverse to pure heart in pure park

German poets in Washington Park
darling sparrows

We can make them
tremble in their sparrowcots

IV

I'll say what no one has said in recent years, Bob Watt is a
major poet. There are singular examples of poets so
unused initially as to make scandal, Fr. Hopkins, Spicer,
Wieners, in Ireland Padraic Fallon and Richard Riordain.
In Watt's case the neglecting blindness is ideological
because he composes stanzas that propel energies and
sentences that blend bite into rhythm. 'Bites' that's the
problem, he attacks people's constructed brain patterns
that have only extremes, practicality and utopia. Readers
cannot handle idea in reverse; satire that's not political
misogyny that's not anti-libido. In fact, his misogyny is
that acute form of reverence known as disguised rapture.
Then there's the fact that hardly a critical soul will touch
a poet without a lot of prior acceptance that stems from
weak cocktail receptions leading to journals/online
backpats.

Watt is an American writer in an older sense, open seismic, gutsy, attached to but wary of transcendence, warm at crossroad in parlor. A village man or woman then a towns man or woman. Whitman or Pound weren't the only examples of these. There was Hart Crane in the drugstore fountain, Niedecker accompanied by grasshopper in Club 26.

Watt is dead in Milwaukee as Beat is dead because the nymphs and the hustlers are not sitting in all night cafes, moonlight is being outsourced. The Writing Programs have won, to write is only to teach to get paid. Muses kick America in the ass.

ON COOKING & JACK SPICER

Graham Mackintosh came to Milwaukee on a later train because his cab had a crash on the way to Union Station in Chicago; one cabbie was black the other Arab and, though there was no damage, they argued.

This was Graham's first visit to the Midwest, though his father worked in California for General Mills. Graham was the second White Rabbit, after Joe Dunn, and devoted his printing life as a publisher to the poet Jack Spicer. He has done work for New Directions, and does the printing for Black Sparrow Press, for John Martin, including the Bukowski volumes. He said Bukowski was a nice man away from his publisher and fans, but an overrated drunk.

Seeing the essence of poetry outside the epic is brevity, even if a repeated brevity, Graham said the important thing about Spicer is he wrote short poems, short books, short letters. 'Jack never wanted to be boring.' 'Early in life Jack had coffee with a little brandy, later brandy with some coffee.' Spicer never got a job in an English Department because he refused to do a PhD under Jo Miles; she blackballed him. He worked under David Read on the Linguistic Atlas of California; he finished that. He would have some lettuce and a roll for lunch 'In the Berkeley Cafeteria you could hear his tray shake as he carried it to the table.'

'He suffered from night blindness and many other ills, all symptoms of alcoholism.'

'Wild Tony Aste from Salt Lake City or Larry Kearney brooding New York Irish had similar status. Jack didn't flirt, he wooed.'

His friend Robert Berg, the San Francisco librarian, had two fifths of gin every night and always got to work. State has an incredible collection of books on food, for many only the wrappers, texts taken home by Berg. 'John Ryan hid two quarts of gin in Berg's oven to stop him drinking; Berg came home with Naomi Frost a faghag; he couldn't find anything to drink but they started cooking: there was a huge explosion. John could never figure out what he did wrong.'

Spicer edited Brautigan's *Trout Fishing in America*; Brautigan really thought he was going to win the Nobel Prize. He was also broke. 'At his divorce hearing his lawyer was convincing the judge how poor Brautigan was, how badly his books were going. Richard jumped up and said his books were selling all over the world. He went broke, his Japanese wife took everything.'

'Wally Hedrik was important for me at CSFA and maybe for Spicer too, that's where I met Jack. Wally was in Gallery 6, the offshoot, with John Ryan. Wally went to Paris and learned to cook, that was how to get on in San Francisco. He made those small machine sculptures all his life. He was a nice guy, anyway everyone wanted a black friend. He lived with Jay DeFeo and gave a party for her 30th birthday. She promised to take her sweater off and she did. That is nothing nowadays but then'

'George Stanley a la Joyce refused to take communion at his brother's ordination to the priesthood. So they hid him in a crowd of nuns who had received the host at an early morning mass. They stayed there in a block; no one noticed George was not in the crowd going to the altar.'

'Jim Alexander and a friend would go to a department store every Saturday to try on bikinis with the help of friendly clerks.'

These are the lives of the poets. Transparencies. When we dead white rabbits arise we will cook up literature again.

The 'G' word

Why didn't I march for you in St. Paul, Minnesota, if I
had, I'd wear Dublin clothes, 'Make out streets safe for
aphorism,' words in Dublin are clothes, I want to be as
frivolous as Auden, 'There may be no body in Ernest but
at least there are clothes.'

There come no more men with old beautiful funds who
stomp like centaurs in bedrooms, stop the lights.

I have been in the business of collecting ideas on the 'G'
word and looking for examples, it's okay to collect
specimens of a word that exists no more. The ideal of
gentleman encourages these characteristics: extensive
talk, inlaid silences, manners when you feel like it, lies
that try to be merciful, talent to sit endlessly in
restaurants, to have the champagne/martini mind (to
think the time of day for them).

Baudelaire a gentleman, so is John Ashbery but Samuel
Beckett was a saint.

A gent is to be a dandy with no dandy virus, an exit sign
present in the world as shadow sipper.

It is immaterial to a gentleman whether in the after-life the Vatican will make him Patron of sparkling wines or simply one of the waiters.

He should only think gingerly of the party city of death, let there be some flowers on the funeral car each of them should be a precedent.

A rewritten manual.

To Joan Navarre on Founding
The Oscar Wilde Society of America

You may not, said Sir Edward Carson to the city cock,
you may not sing of Apollo,
the sun does not shine in England

or Ireland. The city cock
kept stuffing the sun into his brandy glass. Disgusting,
cried Sir Edward, go behind bars.

I am an artist,
the city cock remarked to Sir Edward,
I will lie in the dark with my bright lines.

Cool Tale

You will be judged on good love manners.

Celibate unless in love.

No cold angel stuff here –

be as lonely as an empty champagne bottle if necessary –

the hand in the dish is the history of that,
we are used to the womb
which may outperform the holy spirit – O Sion

seen better looking boys dance in the street,
they had to talk to someone about me
at darts in Champions –

taken for a ride cab ghost city.

Passing St. Hedwig's

he said you should have met me before
I was 21, before girls, I would have gone with you,

this is the end there is no end –

The marine locked him up
in Bayview with recording equipment
he sneaked out on him

not to the Cudahy girl he wrestled in Y Not II
he was moving to Eau Claire to marry her –

went to Kelly high girl of his life
in her wine/Baudelaire Minneapolis boudoir.

Cool tale,
he had to chicken out he was 26.

It was Springbreak no kidding
had been coming over every day,

was en route to New Mexico
Leah was taking him there,

rang from the Bayshore Applebys
his tyre was down, he came over on his doughnut,
got $100 for replacement –

Sneaked away

last safari in eyes them lost safari eyes –

blond boy 18th c. countenance of Tennessee
powdery and enameled surface

with a banjo on his knee,
his head and hair Bardot from the moonshine meadows
played bass too –

there is no end, this is the end –

cool.

Time Present

Adoring the male, what precisely is it
– the young girl in the boy in flower.

PRO DEFUNCTIS

Let us invoke the dead
for five minutes of memory
in pajamas underpants when they took them off.

To Tom Eliot for Publishing and Introducing Nightwood

Lesbians travel in long lines to heaven,
they get there in planes probably flown by male pilots.
God when receiving them does not crossdress but
addresses 'sisters.' God says, 'We are sisters, behind
our body parts we are sisters. You remembered I bring
not the sword but the sword with the kiss. The kiss
however late on your mouth and then on your memory.
In bed at night we talk about cocktails not about beer.'

As they come up the gold stairs,
they exchange their reading lists. They wear Djuna
Barnes's black sweater, driving metaphorically in her two
seater. I invoke chests and nipples, praise to which is due,
let history weigh on the great maturity of women's upper
parts. Jewels on their and our plates. You, undressy God,
bonded us to them, maker of beautiful zones.

I blew ferocious kisses in my youth.
In a dream in 1950 I became a female swan, fondled my
non-reproductive parts, imagined the opera of our loves
on the waterway. It's more beautiful to dive your head as
a swan than to consume cocktails on a yacht: heaven
conveys jarring images. A poem should be a jarring
image projected
in water reflections. Shut your Narcissus face and face the
opposite neck, the other shoulder, the chest, the pearl
opium of desire. So in another dream I turned into Tom

Eliot and magnified as a dark swan of tragic plumage but
swore not to take myself as seriously.

He was by alchemy an inspiring woman
that combination of effects behind older children playing.
Writing an introduction to Djuna's unveiled Lesbian
torture and poetry though she was the one who devised
the speaking male mouth in nightdress. Everyone says
Vespers lying on the ground, live burials.

On a bitter sweet festival of being alive
on the Seine where the rats are slumming, I bring these
bodies, woman and man are animals, let us be unusual.
Tom under his photo of Groucho Marx will point to the
stairs where they are taken up and given God-code,
amulets.

Lady, give anathema to those who fly the flag of any
country except perhaps that of the Knights of Malta & let
the U.N. employ a global hangman to cast into the fire
national emblems including those of the U.N.

Lady, behold a Poet Laureate in each city hall: the
hangmen of poetry.

Lady, correct what is written in the English Department:
'Modernism is sissy, post-Modernism is macho.'

Make us see on Lady Day it is inelegant to be
heterosexual as it was to be a Catholic in Ireland (1955).

The Orchestra of The Age of Enlightenment's instruments
in the void on Lady Day.

Queen of heaven, equate politicians who won't put
'Christianity' in the European Constitution for fear of
praising celibates & politicians who put 'Christianity' into
the American Constitution to soothe rednecks.

House of Ivory, spread Michelangelo's prayer to Amor O
make me see you in every place.

God's Mother, by your well at Cree I stretched summers
ago on the grass and made the rounds and then had
drinks in Reidy's of Cooraclare, gratitude for birth.

God's Mother, I dated you on Madeira en Monte in
summer and you spoke to me all silver over the tomb
vases and crosses of the Emperor Karl and then the vision
reformed and dissolved all day from damp to sun over
Funchal, gratitude for death.

Offertory hymn
I remember the airports full of young soldiers
going to Vietnam – remember Kay Boyle coming
to faculty meetings from Santa Rita where
she had been cleaning the kitchen with Joan Baez
for sitting down in front of an Induction Center.

Now
John Kerry.
Peace heart
peace heart
peace star
peace star.

GRAND JULY

The moon is bigger than the airport
if not naked in July when shall we be naked,
question: naked in daylight or in dark?
This month at night moon-halos!
We should be thrashing in your black sheets
we lack the cruel heart that says follow your heat
in the small ex-hotel
bedroom the bed jutting out to the fridge,
I catch the last kitchen tenderness
Pimm's Cup!

(Dear reviewer of my autobiography,
the helpful material is placed in your department box like
    confetti;
dear Viking, you should be the Arab boy in the corner
    store
who offers the opera it's not too hot to make love.)

In the transmigration of mid-July I am charged
to caress your beauty not fulfill it.
We are idlers with the good kiss
wavering from left or right,
in the middle of our mouths malnutrition is half cured.
You look as if you're Jack Spicer on my back porch
at bar close in filigrees of moon and shadows
you have the same mute godlike magnum eyes that
must get derailed to ship to the moon.

(Dear first and last, we shall all be ghosts without flowers or jewelry, yes, angels and painkillers are just soda drinks, your face carries words.)

ON POPE BENEDICT XV'S ENCYCLICAL

There is spirit
risen and leavened by freedom,
fate of the sweetest. The Roman priest survives
centurion eyes catching absolutely the music.

The pigeons do not fly apart
at the Mass's lightning and
reverberation. Apostolic cantor
Roma: hearts bloom out.

Beneath heaven's eternal dome
I repeat this name
though he who led me to Rome
has poured bliss into twilight.

– Osip Mandelstam

The kingdom of heaven is like 10 virgins going out
in search of a bridegroom, 5 of them drank
gin martinis and 5 of them drank vodka martinis –
looking to the door the bridegroom is expected.
The 5 purer virgins the gin consumers went home
by themselves in cabs, the vodka virgins sped to the
bad wedding feast at their new grooms' apartments.
The commandment comes to: 'Therefore stay awake.'

Matthew 25: 1–13

ALL SOULS DAY

My parents died and are buried
with stone-barmen all around them,
their glasses fill again:
I bring fresh limes to their graves.

NEW YEAR'S EVE

I had a dream that Jim Hazard had put
a poem for me inside a golden biscuit tin.

Note

Father Raymond Roseliep taught at a Catholic university in Dubuque, Iowa, which was known as "Little Rome of the Midwest". He wrote a book on Haiku and published poems in Mary O'Malley's Lyric Theatre Belfast magazine, *Threshold*. One haiku that appeared in the Milwaukee journal, *The Blue Canary*, reads:

> Equal parts
> sky, picasso blood.
> Mix well.